The Financially Healthy Church

Stan J. Tharp, D. Min.

Copyright 2014

Table of Contents

Introduction

Too many churches today are struggling financially! If a church struggles financially, typically, the mission of the church is hindered...and often lost!

The work of the church is too essential to our world to NOT have the resources it needs to thrive! Unfortunately, too many pastors and church leaders don't know how to lead a financially healthy church.

This book is intended to help churches become financially healthy, so they can be free to pursue their God-given mission in our world. One premise of this book is that financial health is *both a blessing and a result of proper practices* for individuals and churches. This book is intended to help you discover or affirm those practices and be blessed.

This book is specifically aimed at helping pastors and church leaders develop and lead financially healthy churches. I have learned the principles in this book through over 30 years of full time pastoral ministry, and an extensive educational background. When followed, these principles help yield significant results that I believe you can experience at your church as well. Being a financially healthy church requires commitment, discipline and sacrifice; but becoming a financially healthy church will bless you, your congregation, and the people you are called to serve beyond your local church.

During my tenure as Lead Pastor at Christian Life Center (CLC), we have seen consistent growth in our general fund (the fund we use to track peoples' tithe and general offering giving). Our giving has grown from $958,828 to $5,063,223 in 24 years. **Our general fund giving has grown in 22 of the past 24 years, in some years by as much as 18%.**

We have seen some amazing things happen in our church giving. For instance, during the 2008-2009 fiscal year, which marked the start of what has been called the worst recession since the great depression, we received $500,000 more in our general fund than budgeted! (The fun part of all that is we gave it all away! We spent $100,000 to send 300,000 fortified rice meals to our partners in Africa. We gave $300,000 to the foreign missionaries we support, to expand their evangelistic reach. We gave $75,000 worth of $5,000 evangelism grants to our inner-city partner churches, and reserved about $25,000 for unexpected benevolence needs within our congregation.)

> While 2008 began what has been called the worst recession since the great depression, we received $500,000 more in our general fund that year than budgeted!

I'm not taking credit for this provision. We depend on God for our resources, and indeed, God is not obligated to bless us financially like He did in 2008. If He wants us to go through financially strenuous times to increase our dependence on Him, He is entitled to do just that.

However, I've learned that there are some fairly simple stewardship principles to follow. If we practice these principles, God tends to provide, and the church remains financially healthy. Please note, "simple" should never be confused with "easy." The principles in this book aren't complicated or hidden, but they do require a disciplined intentionality to be effective.

If your church is having consistent financial struggles, I pray that you will read, share, and apply the principles in this book, and enjoy the financial health that God intends. I say consistent struggles, because we all go through ups and downs of ministry cycles and ongoing fluctuations of the overall economy we live in. Occasional times of financial difficulty are to be expected. However, when financial struggles are ongoing, other concerns may be implicated and need to be addressed.

I believe much financial difficulty in churches could be avoided by following some of the simple proven principles found in this book. You may find that you will want to combine these insights with two other related books I've written: *Teach Them to Give* is a proven tool written to help you apply chapter three of this book, *"Preach It! Every week, and throughout your church."* (See p. 5 of introduction.)

Likewise, the book: *Big...a God-Sized-Vision for Your Church* can help you apply chapter six of this book *"Provision Follows Vision,"* which is a *key* to healthy giving. Our church has found the phrase "Giving follows vision" to be true. The Bible tells us that without a vision, people perish. This is true of a church also. Without a vision, people aren't motivated to give, and churches without a clear compelling vision struggle financially as a result.

As you read this book, I will mention these four additional resources you may want to take advantage of:

1. *Big: A God-Sized Vision* (**https://www.createspace.com/4714835**)

2. *Teach Them to Give* (https://www.createspace.com/4758908)

3. *"The Pipes" Video illustration, available on Createspace and Amazon*

4. *Additional copies of this book: Createspace and Amazon*

If I can be of any assistance to you, please don't hesitate...direct any inquiries to sjtharp1@gmail.com.

Sincerely,

Stan Tharp

Chapter One: A Brief Theology of Stewardship

To be a financially healthy church goes way beyond just having healthy giving. I would argue that healthy giving is an indicator of financial health and a by-product of overall good stewardship. This book could be renamed, the "Healthy Stewardship Practices Church." Below are several Biblically based stewardship principles that guide the practices suggested in this book.

One: The Psalm 24:1 Perspective; It All Belongs to God

According to the Dictionary app on my iPhone, stewardship is defined as: "The position and duties of a steward, a person who acts as the surrogate of another or others, especially by managing property, financial affairs, an estate, etc."[1]

Psalm 24:1 is foundational for a Biblical worldview of proper stewardship:

> "The earth is the Lord's, and all it contains; the world, and those who dwell in it."[2]

Couple the above definition of stewardship with Psalm 24:1 and it becomes clear that everyone pursuing a Biblical worldview should consider themselves as a steward, a surrogate in responsibility, to God. *As such, we realize that "ours" is really "His."* Therefore, we are to consider our material decisions as an expression of our diligence in managing *His money, His property, His possessions, His job,* and so on.

---

[1] Dictionary.com for iPhone

[2] All scripture quotations: New American Standard Version of the Bible. The Lockman Foundation. Anaheim, Ca.: Foundation Publications. 1995.

When Christians give, spend, save, or use, it is of that which is from God, and ultimately belonging to Him all along. The principles and practices of this book (and the companion tool *Teach Them to Give*) are much easier, and make more sense, when we do so from this perspective.

> **When Christians give, spend, save, or use, it is of that which is from God, and ultimately belonging to Him all along.**

In a secondary level of stewardship responsibility, pastors and church leaders should see themselves as "acting as the surrogate of another" in managing church finances, property, equipment, etc. Not only do these resources belong to God, **they have been given** in obedient, sacrificial good-faith, by members of the church. Such stewardship isn't just the responsibility of board members and pastors. Volunteer children's teachers should use supplies responsibly, youth workers must spend funds appropriately, and each person should act wisely when it comes to spending and using church resources.

Two: The 2 Corinthians 8 Principle; Diligent Financial Management

These verses became a guiding principle for me when I served as the Ministry Administrator for Christian Life Center, and have remained so for me as Lead Pastor to this day:

> "...taking precaution so that no one will discredit us in our administration of this generous gift; for we have regard for what is honorable, not only in the

sight of the Lord, but also in the sight of men."
(vs. 20, 21)

In this passage, the Apostle Paul is speaking of the generous offering the church gave him in support of the work of spreading the Gospel. Paul makes us aware of two very important dimensions of responsibility. *First, leaders must handle financial concerns of the church knowing that it is indeed "God's money."* Ideally, this awareness in itself should be enough to motivate leaders to do an exemplary job of stewardship.

Every Christian can acknowledge that just because we know God is going to hold us accountable, doesn't mean it guarantees our proper conduct. If it did, we as Christians would never tell a lie, lust, lose our tempers, envy, hold a grudge, use wrong language, or gossip.

Unfortunately, and tragically, many church leaders have found themselves in horrendous situations because they were inappropriate stewards of "God's money" even though they knew someday they would be accountable to God for such wrongdoing. Somehow, such divine "someday-accountability" isn't enough to keep our behavior appropriate at all times.

To raise the bar on accountability, Paul adds the standard of human expectations:

"We have regard for what is honorable...**in the sight of men**."

Since I have an MBA as part of my education, this verse has been easy to understand. I believe church leaders should handle finances in a way that even an outside CPA would approve. I'm not necessarily suggesting all churches get financial audits (they can be very costly), *however, I do believe we should make financial decisions and follow financial practices that are "honorable" to contemporary expectations of financial accountability and responsibility.*

I have a sense of accountability to "the person in the pew." I respect that the people who attend our church are making financial sacrifices to tithe and give offerings to support the ministries we are called to serve. Some people work more than one job to make ends meet, yet they are dutiful to always honor God first in their giving. I want to conduct our finances in a way that I can give an honest, accountable answer to them for how we manage, as Paul calls it, **"[their] most generous gift."**

Three: The Matthew 25: 14-29 Principles; The Hard Work and Rewards of Spending Well

There are at least four important stewardship principles in this famous passage.

FIRST: GOD IS AN ACCOUNTABILITY GOD.

Notice that these are the words of Jesus. The "man/master who goes on a journey" represents Christ. In this story, the master returns, and asks the slaves to give an account of what they did with their master's money. Similarly, **all who are in a position of leadership responsibility to manage money given to the work of Christ must expect a time when Christ will "settle accounts" with us for our stewardship.**

SECOND: OPPORTUNITY GROWS AS WE PROVE DILIGENT TO GROW IN RESPONSIBILITY

Jesus gave the different servants different amounts, according to their individual abilities. It is important for us to realize we must avoid comparisons to others, as in "Why don't I get the opportunity they do?" God knows what we are capable of.

It is also important to note that the steward who ended up with 10 talents didn't start out that way. Nor did the "four talent" steward start with four, he proved himself faithful with two first. As we are responsible with what we have, God will then increase it to more. The "Faithful over little/Faithful over much" premise is pretty non-negotiable. Seldom, if ever, do you see someone "starting at the top", whether this be in the church world or in business realms. However, as we are faithful stewards of the opportunities given to us and maximize that potential, God trusts us with the next step of "more." This applies to ministry opportunity, financial provisions, etc. Jesus summarizes it this way in Luke 16:10-12:

"He who is faithful in a little thing is faithful also in much; and he who is unrighteous in a very little thing is unrighteous also in much. Therefore if you have not been faithful in the use of unrighteous wealth, who will entrust the

Intentionality is an underlying key to effective financial management, both in spending and growing ministry income.

true riches to you? And if you have not been faithful in the use of that which is another's, who will give you that which is your own?"

THIRD: IT TAKES A LOT OF WORK TO SPEND MONEY WELL

The two servants who are exemplary in this story "gained more" for their master. The one servant who is the bad example is called wicked and "lazy" for not gaining a return on their master's resources. The word gained means "to work to earn a profit." In all my years of church ministry, and the countless financial reports I've worked with, I have made a curious observation. By looking at a budget report, I can usually tell if an area of ministry in our church is doing well or not. Budgets are tools. They help us plan on spending and receiving money,

financial activity is a monetary representation of what is actually happening in ministry activity. I have consistently observed that if a ministry is diligent in the planning of their ministry activity (goal setting), and then they effectively accomplish those plans, financial activity tends to reflect the same.

The larger the amount of money, the more hard work it takes to spend it well in accordance with goal-directed plans, resulting in ministry growth and gains. This is a helpful caution to those who "budget big." To whom much is given (budgeted), much is going to be required in terms of ministry effectiveness. To those who feel such performance-evaluation type of accountability isn't appropriate for ministry, Jesus would tend to disagree.

As He told the story, Jesus included the accountability dimension:

> *"Now after a long time the master of those slaves came and settled accounts with them...his master said to him, 'Well done, good and faithful servant, you were faithful with few things, I will put you in charge of many..."* Matthew 25: 19, 21

Ministry leaders need to remain mindful that they are funded by the financially sacrificial obedience of those they lead. The money entrusted to us should be turned into "kingdom gains" with God's prayerfully added blessing.

FOURTH: IT WILL BE WORTH IT ALL SOME DAY!

Not only do the "faithful stewards" receive more opportunity to serve their master ("...you were faithful over few things, I will put you in charge of many things..."); they will also receive a joyful reward ("Well done...enter into the joy of your master."). We must never underestimate what it will be like when we receive the divine affirmation and reward of a work well done for our Lord, Master and Savior, Jesus Christ. (Matthew 25:21, 2 Co. 5:10, Rev. 22:12).

Four: Plan Wisely; Follow Proverbs 15:22 and Luke 14: 28-31

For the most part, healthy stewardship is seldom spontaneous. **Intentionality is an underlying key to effective financial management, both in spending and growing ministry income.** Verses like Proverbs 15:22 make a well-thought out budget a prerequisite to healthy finances:

> *"Without consultation, plans are frustrated, but with many counselors they succeed."*

Jesus likewise affirms sound financial planning in Luke 14, where the person who begins a building project (a tower) without proper budgeting will be considered a fool and jeopardizes the success of the entire endeavor. When we are responsible for spending God's money we must anticipate the amount of income we hope to receive, *and* we must anticipate the intended uses for these resources. Far too many pastors and church leaders operate spontaneously under the attitude of, "If we have it, we can spend it." This is far from the 2 Corinthians 8 "Diligent Financial Management" principle mentioned earlier.

Income must be planned for. Not only should we anticipate the amounts of income we plan to receive, we should also anticipate the sources for that income. For churches, sources typically include offerings, occasional fund-raisers, fees charged (for instance, the kids' ministry is taking a trip to the zoo, requiring an admission fee), and so on.

Likewise, expenditures for anticipated income need to be properly planned. In the accounting world, **operating expenses** refer to those costs of "doing ministry" in an ongoing fashion, from paying the church light bills, to staff salaries and children's ministry supplies. **Capital expenses** refer to the cost of buildings and to purchase vehicles or major equipment.

Unfortunately, many churches and ministries fail to budget wisely by not planning for the capital side of their budget. I remember serving on the board of a ministry that owned a large office building from which they operated. My first exposure to the budget alarmed me: they didn't even have a capital budget. I recall asking "how are you planning for the future costs of taking care of the building and property?" After all, air-conditioners wear out, parking lots need to be re-surfaced, and eventually, carpet needs to be replaced. I'm glad to say they have since added this important part of their budget.

> We spend money as we planned. If we budget money, say, for utilities, we don't spend those funds on decorating the sanctuary. ..You spend it as you planned it, or you don't spend it at all.

The ministry or church that fails to set aside funds for the upkeep of their facilities and equipment is not practicing the kind of wise stewardship the Bible encourages. They are simply postponing a potential financial crisis.

It is also important to be sure to follow through on budget intentions. I have always been adamant about planning our income and our expenditures. Once wisely budgeted (and approved), we spend money as we planned. If we budget money, say, for utilities, we don't spend those funds on decorating the sanctuary. Likewise, just because we may have more money than anticipated in our education budget, doesn't mean we take those funds and use them to hire another staff person or to give raises. You spend it as you planned to spend it, or you don't spend it at all.

This may sound inflexible, but I've seen far too many churches do otherwise and end up in trouble. I am also a proponent of having an annual budget that is approved by the church governing body. For us, our church board approves our proposed budget for the coming year, they recommend the budget to the congregation, and the congregation votes to approve the budget at an annual meeting. **Once approved, integrity is sustained and trust is built, as the people who do the spending match the expectations of those who did the original "approving."**

Remember the definition of a steward is to act as a "surrogate" of those who give in the offering, to manage their money, church facilities,

> The ministry or church that fails to set aside funds for the upkeep of their facilities and equipment is not practicing the kind of wise stewardship the Bible encourages. They are postponing a potential financial crisis.

equipment, supplies, and so on. *To earn the trust of those we ask to follow us in ministry and in giving, we must do the following:*

1. Clearly show them we plan wisely for anticipated income and expenditures.

2. Communicate these intentions to them (usually through a budget) and ask them to affirm those plans as in keeping with the overall purpose/vision toward which they feel they are being asked to give.

3. Periodically (most often annually) we need to demonstrate that how we told them we were going to spend the money is generally what happened.

4. We must demonstrate that we are "stewarding" the financial activity and well-being of the church in a way that sustains the long-term fiscal health of the ministry.

I have found a direct correlation between how much givers trust their leaders and how healthy financial giving is to a ministry. Furthermore, I have found that the more people are motivated by the overall mission of the ministry, the healthier the giving is to that ministry.

I have experienced this first-hand at our church. Several years ago, after launching our "God-Sized Vision," **a woman came up to me and said what I imagine every pastor longs to hear: "Pastor, I just LOVE tithing to this church!"** You'll hear more about this in the final chapter, "Pro-vision follows vision." I suggest you read a copy of my book *"BIG: A God-Sized Vision for Your Church"* for help in discerning healthy direction for your church.

Chapter Two: Preach It! (Every Year)

I remember before I was convinced of the principles of church financial health.

I knew I was supposed to preach on giving, and would occasionally try to muster up the courage to do so, especially if offerings had been consistently below budget and a well-intentioned board member suggested that I preach on the subject.

I would preach about giving, usually in the form of one point embedded in a sermon on a related topic. I'd land briefly (and awkwardly) on why people should give. I'd feel my anxiety rise as I would watch the arm-crossing non-verbal's of disapproval from defensive congregants.

> I remember the day I was reflecting on the words of Jesus, and the state of our culture, and I felt convicted that I must never preach on giving and stewardship in such a half-hearted way again.

I would finish my point, and with relief to all in the room (myself included), I would move on to the rest of the message feeling that I had "done my part" in addressing the need for Christians to give.

Thankfully, all that changed. I felt too disturbed to continue avoiding the subject. One day, as I was reflecting on the words of Jesus and the state of our culture, I felt convicted that I must never preach on giving and stewardship in such a half-hearted way again.

Jesus himself said that money can become a god that people worship, and that it can lead them to an eternity in hell. That sounds harsh, but if we believe "you cannot serve God and money," it must be true (Matthew 6:24). In that same sentence, Jesus tells us that we can serve only one master— either God or money. The potential disposition toward these two possible masters is frightful. It is not neutral. If I serve money, then I'll hate God, *or I can serve God, and never see money as more than a blessing from Him and a tool to steward as He directs.* Jesus said you're going to serve either Him or money.

Ironically, I had way less apprehension about preaching what the Bible says about sex, than I did about money.

As I thought further about our culture, I realized that perhaps the two greatest distractions away from our faith are materialism and sensuality. We are bombarded daily with messages about consumerism and sex as advertisers skillfully create and encourage an insatiable desire for both sexual pleasure and material things. In fact, the two are combined together so often that most of us have heard the advertising axiom, "sex sells."

It is then that I realized I have a responsibility to preach God's word in both these areas. Ironically, I had way less apprehension about preaching what the Bible says about sex than I did about money. **Yet, if I believe the words of Christ, I must preach both. Like a good family doctor, I must bear a two-fold message, of prevention and "cure" regarding our financial, material world.** If I don't teach our congregation a proper perspective on money and things, our culture will shape this part of their world view, and **the results can be disastrous.**

The apostle Paul poses a rhetorical question in Romans about the gospel message that also applies to Biblical principles of stewardship: if pastors don't preach about it, how will people know?

If pastors don't preach regularly about money and possessions, Christians will adopt the views of our surrounding culture, which place an undue emphasis on the value of money and things.

> *"How then will they call on Him in whom they have not believed? How will they believe in Him whom they have not heard? And how will they hear without a preacher?" Romans 10:14*

Americans currently live in the most financially prosperous nation in history. Materialism abounds as advertisers give us endless suggestions for what to do with our money and relentlessly try to convince us of what possessions we must have.

If pastors don't regularly preach about money and possessions, Christians will adopt the views of our surrounding culture, which places an undue emphasis on the value of money and things. This sets people up for lives of discontent and a constant chasing after that which is nice, but won't truly satisfy. Consequently, I realized that I must be the one who preaches a Biblically compatible view of stewardship to our church. If not, the people I lead may go beyond consumerism to worshipping the god of money and despising the God of truth.

> For the Christian pursuing a Biblical world-view, the financial and material side of our lives should be relatively 'stress-free.'

For the Christian pursuing a Biblical world-view, the financial and material side of our lives should be relatively 'stress-free' and marked by an internal state of well-being that the Bible calls contentment. **Think of taking a deep breath, and exhaling in a relaxing "Ahhhhhhh." That is the feeling we should have about the stuff and money in our lives.** Contemporary studies find this state of well-being to be far from the truth as financial stress is often paramount in peoples' lives. Sadly, most financial stress can be avoided by knowing and following a Biblical approach to our finances and things.

Preaching healthy financial practices is a must for any Biblically motivated pastor and church. In addition to what is taught publicly from the platform, additional learning environments are necessary. We currently offer a classroom setting of the video course "Financial Peace University" by Dave Ramsey, for people who want to "dig deeper." We also have a few individuals in our church available for one-on-one financial counseling for those interested. We encourage healthy stewardship teaching across the age spectrum as well, in both our children's and youth ministries. This is a practical example of the Biblical admonition to "train up a child" in the ways they should go.

Before suggesting the kind of sermons you should preach, let me be clear and give you two reasons why you *shouldn't* preach on stewardship. **First,** you should not preach on stewardship as a means to get more money in the church offerings. **Second,** you should not preach on stewardship so people live a more lavish lifestyle (have more money and get more stuff). While Biblical stewardship principles will indeed result in both greater church income and a variety of blessings in the lives of those who are obedient, *stewardship should be preached because it is part of a Biblical world view that honors God.*

> Before suggesting the kind of sermons you SHOULD preach, let me be clear and give you two reasons why you SHOULDN'T preach on stewardship.

You may ask, "**What am I supposed to preach?**" Below is a suggested list of thoughts/truths that can be incorporated into a sermon series on stewardship. I would suggest preaching a 2 to 4 week series on stewardship every year, at different times of the year (the longest I think I have preached is a 4 week series). But be sure to make the series something people actually enjoy and look forward to!

First: Proverbs 3:5-10 Stewardship is a matter of trust. If we indeed trust God with all our heart, according to this passage, it is good for us emotionally, physically, mentally, financially, relationally, and practically.

A. The real question then is **not** "How much we should give, save, spend, etc.?" The question is: "Do we really trust God enough to live our financial lives His way?"

B. If you currently aren't living your financial life God's way, it will take time to learn, practice and benefit from doing so. You didn't get into a financial mess overnight; it will take time to "fix it."

Second: Psalm 24:1 Everything belongs to God.

A. If we truly believe this, then we don't honestly own anything. We are simply stewards of what belongs to God.

B. We need to be concerned with the questions, "How does God want us to manage His money and His stuff? What attitude does He want me to have toward them?"

Third: Matthew 6:31-34 God can be trusted. If indeed He knows our needs ahead of time, do we trust him to provide for us, while we are being obedient to Him?

26

Fourth: Deuteronomy 8: 17-18 God provides my earning ability. Not only does my paycheck belong to God; God can be trusted because He gave me the ability to earn it in the first place. With this perspective, I don't give grudgingly, I give gratefully!

Fifth: Matthew 6: 33 God has a plan.

    A.   Seek God first.

    B.   He can be trusted to provide what follows.

Finally: John 10: 10 Satan has a counterfeit plan.

    A.   Since the Garden of Eden, whatever God means for good, Satan tries to use against us. (Think Marriage, family, material world, etc.)

    B.   Owning through debt is a great counterfeit of contentment. Prov. 22:7

It is one thing to share Biblical principles regarding stewardship and our everyday lives. The helpful pastor must go beyond this "head knowledge" and provide helpful practical financial behaviors based on this teaching. **Learn and Practice the principles of Healthy Stewardship:** A few are suggested below:

    A.   **Pay Your Taxes:** Matthew 22: 15-22 the average American pays somewhere around 28% of their income in taxes.

    B.   **Pay God:** Matthew: 22:15-22 It is noteworthy that in the phrase, "Render to Caesar the things that are Caesar's and render to God the things that are God's" Jesus uses the same word, whether we are paying taxes to the government or giving to God. For Christ, what we give to God is no less mandatory than what we "give" in taxes to the government. A quick internet search will reveal the average American (including church-goers) gives just over 2% of their income to charity. Christians should add at least 10% to this, since the Bible consistently talks about giving "tithes (tenth) and offerings."

This often raises another question; "Do I tithe off of gross income, or net?" I believe according to Matthew 22: 21 that we tithe off of our gross income, what belongs to God

> **As such, they commit the Malachi 3:8-10 offense, and "rob God."**

is a totally separate issue from what belongs to "Caesar."

C. **Pay Yourself:** Proverbs 21:20 tells us that saving is sound financial wisdom. Whether to replace major purchases someday (no one ever bought an 'eternal set of tires'), or planning ahead for retirement, 10% is a good savings goal.

D. **Choose your lifestyle:** Philippians 4:11, Proverbs 30:7-9 If you do the math, 28% to taxes, plus at least 12% in giving, plus 10% in savings...leaves the average American 50% of their gross income to live on. This is possible, if we learn to be content with what we have.

E. **Avoid Debt:** Proverbs 22:7, Psalm 37:21 Sadly, the average American spends as much as 30% of their income on servicing debt. While people may question this, for many, a third of their check is easily gone after paying credit card and auto payments.

With this level of debt, people typically say they "would love to give, but I just can't afford to." As such, they commit the Malachi 3:8-10 offense, and "rob God."

As a reminder, when preaching on healthy financial practices (Biblical Stewardship), do your homework. Some internet searches will reveal interesting statistics about debt, spending, saving and giving habits common today, and in your community. Be creative! Find memorable ways to illustrate your points. Likewise, internet searches can provide you with examples of stewardship sermons that can inspire you for your congregation.

Pastor friends who have used this illustration, and preached an accompanying sermon series (visit clcdayton.com) have consistently reported dramatic increases in giving...from the 10-40% range, all the way to income doubling!

Also, keep in mind that stewardship sermons should not be confused with the prosperity teachings so popular today. Stewardship is not how to get what we want in order to live extravagantly. *Stewardship is a lifestyle that honors God with what He has given to us. It includes being content with what we have, wise with what we earn, and enjoying being blessed by God to be a blessing to others.* While I believe obedience to Biblical principles brings blessings, it's hard for me to preach wealth through giving, from the words of one who told us to store our treasures in heaven, not on Earth.

Be creative. Use illustrations to communicate about stewardship. During a past series, we had a recliner on stage. As I sat in it, and

> When preaching on healthy financial practices (Biblical Stewardship), do your homework. Some internet searches will reveal interesting statistics...

began talking about "the comfortable bondage of debt" a couple of guys came up and put several huge, heavy chains on me. By the time they were done, we created a word-picture: getting into debt may be comfortable (a new car, new furniture, new whatever), but over time, Proverbs 22:7 comes true and the borrower becomes slave to the lender.

I like to use a lot of illustrations when I preach. In fact**, the most requested sermon illustration of any sermon series I have ever preached is a stewardship illustration** known to our congregation of a few thousand people...simply as "The Pipes." If it seems like I have gone too long without preaching on stewardship, people who have begun to practice these Biblical principles and experienced the blessings of obedience will literally ask me, **"Pastor Stan, when are you going to preach 'The Pipes' again?"**

If you'd like to use this illustration, you may download a video of it to adapt for your teaching at amazon.com. I highly recommend checking it out. People who've watched the illustration consistently comment that there is something about those PVC pipes, and "moving them around like that," which makes a lasting impression that motivates people toward proper stewardship. Pastor friends who have used that illustration and preached an accompanying sermon series have consistently reported dramatic increases in giving from the 10-40% range, all the way to income doubling!

> I can't stress enough...the reason for preaching the principles and practice of healthy Biblical stewardship is NOT to get people to give more in an offering.

I can't stress enough that the reason for preaching the principles and practices of healthy Biblical stewardship is not to get people to give more in an offering. Increased giving is a healthy by-product. If your motivation is just to improve the church budget, your preaching is likely going to be manipulative.

The motivation for preaching on healthy Biblical stewardship is because it is beneficial for your congregation spiritually. Not only is it good for people spiritually to practice Biblical stewardship, it is dangerous for them not to. If I am ever tempted to avoid teaching on stewardship, I am motivated by the example of Jesus. He used some pretty strong words about our relationship with money and things. It was Jesus who said you can't serve (love) both God and money.

I stopped to think about these powerful, confrontational words. It didn't sound like a theology where Jesus wants to make me rich and impose as few financial demands on me

> ...one of our greatest temptations AWAY from our faith is our money and our stuff.

as possible. Proper stewardship requires a sense of responsibility. The words of Christ, coupled with the rest of the New Testament, made me realize the dangers of living in a financially prosperous nation...one of our greatest temptations AWAY from our faith is our money and our stuff. Responsible pastors must preach to help their congregation avoid such pitfalls.

Don't preach stewardship to increase giving. Pray, seek God, and study His word until you are motivated to preach stewardship for the health and well-being of those you lead.

Chapter Three: Preach it! Every Week, Throughout Your Church

While is it important to creatively preach healthy stewardship on an annual basis for 2 to 4 weeks each year, that won't be enough. People in your congregation are bombarded on a daily basis by countless marketing messages that promote discontentment. Nothing in our current culture supports the principles of Biblical stewardship in their daily lives. **Knowing this, it is obvious that a once-a-year series, however motivating, won't have the "staying power" to promote life change that people will practice permanently.**

> To accomplish anything lasting in your church, like healthy stewardship practices, requires more than just a "top-down" approach to communication and change. You need a way to communicate truth that will travel throughout the body of your church.

I believe healthy stewardship needs what I call a "systemic influence." Let me explain by recalling my late, good friend Emerson Steck. When I first joined the staff at Christian Life Center, I was responsible for the buildings and grounds (among a lot of other things). We have a drainage ditch at the church that runs across the property, close to the main building.

In the spring, it flows and looks like a creek. But by mid-summer, all water is gone, and it becomes a muddy, mucky, ditch at best. By August every year, weeds run rampant and it is an unsightly mess. As much as our staff and volunteers would try to cut the weeds back, they always returned.

Emerson lived in a nearby rural community and was familiar with farming enough to tell me that he had the solution for all of the weeds. "It's called 'Roundup'" he said. Emerson told me of this amazing herbicide that only requires a touch on a single leaf of those pesky weeds and it would go throughout the plant, even to the root system, and kill it. In fact, Emerson guaranteed it!

> **Each week the offering time should include an intentional time of teaching about giving.**

Well, I couldn't refuse an offer like that, so Emerson bought some Roundup, volunteered some time, and sure enough, in a few weeks the weeds were dead. This is not because Emerson coated every part of the plants or pulled out all the roots. Instead, he simply took a weed killer that was "systemic" and touched the unwanted weeds with it. This contact caused the chemical to travel "systemically" throughout the plant and do its work.

To accomplish anything lasting in your church, like healthy stewardship practices, requires more than just a preaching approach to communication and change. You need a "systemic" way to communicate truth that will travel throughout the body of your church, from the top to the roots, so-to-speak, just as roundup did in those weeds. You need to communicate stewardship from the platform in the sanctuary, as well as in the children's classes. It needs to be practiced by volunteer youth workers, and church elders. Likewise, teachers or small group leaders need to model and teach stewardship to adults, children and youth alike!

Teach a mini-segment on giving each weekend in your weekly worship service.

I firmly believe that when it is time in the service to receive the offering, *it shouldn't be a time that gets cluttered with announcements about church socials or youth activities.* While announcements may need to be made, the weekly offering time should include an intentional moment of teaching about giving. It only needs to be about two minutes long, but the mini-teaching should include a Biblical reference and an appropriate, practical perspective on giving.

> Such weekly reminders are a necessary antidote to our societal "dis-ease" of discontentment.

This constant but brief training is an ongoing public reinforcement of the teachings in your annual stewardship sermon series. By keeping this ever before the congregation, you publicly and consistently help shape values and attitudes about stewardship and giving. We are bombarded daily by countless messages about what we don't have and must get. Weekly offering teachings serve as reminders that are a necessary antidote to our societal disease of discontentment. I believe, over time, that there is a noticeable correlation between weekly giving and the quality of the thoughts about giving that are shared at the offering invitation.

This may seem to be a difficult habit to develop, but once you are committed to this practice it comes easier.

As mentioned earlier, I have written a book that our staff and lay leaders have used for years to help them come up with "offering ideas" for the weekly service. It is called *"Teach Them to Give"*. (See page 5 of the introduction).

Below is a sample from the book to help you picture the kind of offering teaching I'm suggesting:

NOT TOO POOR, NOT TOO RICH

"Give me neither poverty nor riches, feed me with the food that is my portion, lest I be full and deny you and say 'Who is the Lord?' Or lest I be in want and steal, and profane the name of my God."

Proverbs 30: 8, 9

Most of us would have no trouble identifying that we do not consider ourselves "too rich." More than likely, all of us would like more financial resources than we have. Yet, at the same time, we must honestly admit that we are not "too poor" either.

Indeed, by the world's standards, even the poor American is a fortunate citizen of the global society. Studies show that if you make a combined household income of over $20,000, you are among the top 10% of wage-earners in the world. The wisdom of Proverbs encourages us to find an "in the middle" place...and be comfortably content living there.

If you aren't too rich, and you really aren't too poor, be thankful. Both of these financial extremes can be difficult to live with and still maintain a proper relationship with God. Giving is a way in which we demonstrate our contentment with what we have.

Because you don't have too much...because you don't have too little...give. Give to Him who blessed you "in the middle."

Find ways to teach and practice healthy Biblical stewardship throughout the ages of your church.

Be sure that stewardship principles are taught in age appropriate ways at all levels of your congregation. The rationale for this is simple: from how you brush your teeth, display good manners, or drive a car, we learn life-long practices in our childhood and youth. Healthy biblical stewardship is no different. Even the Bible tells us to train up a child in the way they should go so that when they get older, they stay at it! (Proverbs 22:6).

Kids can learn about tithing. I know I did, and I've been

> Kids and youth need to know that all they own is entrusted to them by God. Teach them that things are a blessing to be 'held loosely, taken care of and enjoyed, but not loved.'

doing it for decades since! Children and youth need to know that all they own is entrusted to them by God. Teach them that things are a blessing to be held loosely, taken care of, and enjoyed, but not loved. These same principles should be communicated to your youth; and as they begin to develop earning ability, tithing and giving should be part of their spiritual practices.

The giving part of stewardship isn't just for youth once they begin to get part-time jobs. I have seen the kids at our church come alive with excitement and also raise thousands of dollars to do everything from help buy small farm animals for villagers in Swaziland, Africa, to providing school supplies for poor children in Dayton, Ohio. The greatest thing is that they learn the joy of the truth of scripture that it is "more blessed to give than to receive" (Acts 20:35).

Find ways to teach healthy Biblical stewardship principles in classes or small group settings for adults.

In addition to annual sermons on healthy Biblical stewardship, you'll want to provide at least occasional classes or small group trainings for adults wanting to grow in stewardship. Through the years, we have used great materials from Larry Burkett, Ron Blue, and most recently, Dave Ramsey.

The key is to find a curriculum that fits your church and to make learning available. If possible, try to time the start of such classes or groups with sermon series' on stewardship. I recently did a two week series, and it was followed by a three week mini-version of our stewardship class that was attended by a couple dozen people. If you project the potential impact of 12 to 15 households from your congregation beginning to practice Biblical stewardship, it will have a lifelong impact on their family, and make a significant impact on your church!

You may also want to develop a few individuals or couples within your church who can be referred to for people with complicated situations or detailed questions. Norm is one of those people in our church. He is a semi-retired CPA, has served in a variety of leadership roles in our church throughout the years, and I can always call on him to help people with complicated "financial messes." He kindly, but firmly, guides them through the tough choices on their way to healthy Biblical stewardship.

Chapter Four: Practice What You Preach...As a Church

To practice good stewardship as leaders of the church means we are intentional about our finances. We have a defined budget process, budget writing season, and extensive rationale for funds requested in our budget. Once approved by our board and our congregation (at our annual council meeting), we produce monthly report updates for leaders and staff to review in order to stay in touch with how our budget management is going.

> Too many churches get into trouble by spending money that never "comes in."

1. **The first step in proper stewardship practices is to prayerfully anticipate income as accurately as possible, and build a budget.** Churches usually only have a few income sources. Typically, there is the primary donation fund which, according to the theology of this book, would consist of tithes giving. Some churches choose to build their budget on an annual pledge basis. Whatever your approach, this "general fund" is typically the primary source of funding.

Additional income may come from fund-raising projects, fees for activities, and so on. The important thing to note is that the projected income for the coming year needs to be fairly accurate. If income is less than anticipated, expenditures will need to be adjusted accordingly. Too many churches get into trouble by spending money that never "comes in."

We have found that our income is somewhat predictable. Our fiscal year begins September 1. We typically budget an annual increase in giving between three and eight percent. As a result, from September until late November, our total giving tends to run a little behind the budget target. However, as attendance and stewardship practices grow during the year, the budget grows as well. By the end of our fiscal year, we are usually at, or ahead of the projected budget income.

> The "use" we budget for funds is as important as the amount we budget for the various uses. If we didn't budget for an expense ahead of time, we usually don't spend it.

HOWEVER, if our budget continues to lag, we adjust spending plans. On more than one occasion, we have sent memos to our staff instructing them "If you don't absolutely need it, don't spend it (until giving gets more in line with our projections)." Typically, we "pull in our belts", then, as the budget comes along, we ease restrictions and continue to move forward. Even these "tighten up" times are healthy for us. We have often found expenditures we don't really need to make and come to appreciate our resources even more.

2. **We have found that the second important leadership practice is to plan your spending, and then follow your plan.** As part of our budgeting process, we make a detailed list of expenses by category. Then, as we look ahead at the activities for the year, we plan what month we anticipate spending them. We also provide a statement or two about why these funds are necessary or how they will be spent. This rationale further assures us that we are asking for funds that are indeed needed, and that there is a ministry-related plan driving these financial decisions.

    For example, a typical line of rationale in the youth budget may be something like this:

    Supplies: $150 per month for "Extreme games" outreach effort. Once a month (except for December and July) we plan an Extreme/Olympic type of competition for youth to bring their friends. This money buys game supplies and light refreshments for each event. ANNUAL TOTAL: $1,500

    In this regard, it is important to spend funds as we said we were going to spend them. For example, if we have underspent in a particular fund, say supplies and equipment, but we are at budget in the salary account, we don't feel free to hire additional staff by taking from the supplies account "just because we have money there." The "use" we budget funds for is as important as the amount we budget for the various uses. If we didn't budget for it, we usually don't spend it.

    This approach to income and spending helps people know they can trust us. Strong trust is a prerequisite to healthy

giving. People won't give to a church whose leaders can't be trusted to manage contributions in a way that *"is honorable in the sight of men."* Below are examples of practices that grow the financial trust of a congregation in their leaders:

a. If they know the budget they approve is founded on sound rationale, and will be followed accordingly, **trust grows.**

b. If the congregation knows that expenses are projected as accurately as possible throughout the coming year, **trust grows.**

c. If people know that both expenses and income will be monitored on a regular basis, and that adjustments will be made if income falls short, **trust grows**.

d. To reflect on the words of Jesus, if people know your fiscal "yes is yes, and your no is no," **trust will grow.** (Matthew 5:37)

> We quickly developed a plan to retire our debt aggressively. We trimmed our budget and learned to live within our means. The credit line became unnecessary.

3. **It seems like this should go without saying, but proper stewardship also requires sound bookkeeping and financial**

practices. Shop for the best value. Get more than one bid on large purchases. Keep good, easy to read financial records. Pay your bills on time. *Those who handle the financial records should keep in mind: you represent the church, and ultimately, God. Vendors will be watching and forming (or re-enforcing) their opinions of churches and Christians based on your prompt payment and healthy financial practices.*

4. **Avoid Debt whenever possible.** The stewardship outline in chapter two quotes Proverbs 22:7 while stating that debt should be avoided. I had recently become the Lead Pastor of our church when we first got serious about stewardship at the level of our church board. We were carrying debt on our building, as well as debt on a line of credit, just to "make ends meet." At the time, we were already teaching a class to congregants about stewardship, including the value of "avoiding debt." I remember our discussion and conviction that we needed to "practice what we preached."

> **Healthy stewardship practices through the years have enabled us to do things in the past 5 years that we could have only dreamed of...**

We quickly developed a plan to retire our debt aggressively. We also trimmed our budget, and learned to live within our means. The credit line soon became unnecessary. We began to truly practice the budget principles mentioned above, and learned to be content with what God provided our church through giving, and to do ministry within that provision.

5. **Aim to develop a stewardship-minded culture at your church.** This includes preaching more consistently on stewardship, and then practicing what you preach. When stewardship is part of your culture, it helps grow the awareness and obedience of the congregation. Over time, this has empowered our church to do things we would have only dreamed of. In the final chapter, "Provision follows vision" I'll share some financial accomplishments that would have been impossible for us before we became a "stewardship-minded culture" and got serious about stewardship.

6. **Avoid "emergency offerings."** This stewardship practice is SO important. Many churches often take "special offerings" as though driven by a sense of emergency, for non-emergencies. For example, the pastor gets up and pleads, "We need to take a special offering, the furnace finally went out, and if we don't raise the funds, we're not going to have heat when winter comes next month!"

> **This kind of urgency is really poor stewardship in disguise.** Planning ahead is part of healthy stewardship. Planning ahead helps consumers anticipate and save for major purchases, rather than go into unnecessary debt. As such, it is vital that church leaders also anticipate expenses and plan ahead. In the example given, it is no surprise that a 30 year old furnace finally "died." Whether it is furnaces, parking lots, or copiers, none of them are eternal. No salesman ever said, "This is the last one you will ever have to buy." *This begs the obvious question,* "Then why don't church leaders plan ahead for when things need to be replaced, maintained or fixed?"

When a pastor or board member gets up in front of a congregation and issues an urgent plea for a need that could (and should) have been financially anticipated and planned for, it goes against the wisdom of Proverbs 21:20 that tells us saving for future needs (like a worn out furnace) is wisdom! As you plan ahead to maintain and replace equipment, keep up the facilities, and so on, a key ingredient to stewardship improves in your church...**trust grows!**

7. Say "Thank you" to people for giving! Everyone likes to be appreciated. Everyone likes to feel they are making a valuable contribution, whether it is to a workplace, school, community, family, a friendship, or to their church. Be appreciative of people as they give. I try to say "thank you for giving" as we begin to receive the offering. Likewise, send regular contribution statements that summarize giving and include a note of thanks with the statement.

In addition to these more common means of expression, about two years ago I began a very personal way to say thank you that I would challenge pastors to try. I have begun asking our bookkeeper to send my administrative assistant the names of people who appear to be tithing (I let her use her judgment). We invite them to my office for an hour of coffee and dessert on Wednesday evenings. The purpose of our social time is simple, and I explain it to my guests (We usually invite about 6 people to sit around my conference table for these 'thank-you desserts'). I have no hesitation saying "thank-you" to people who give their time in volunteering in the church. However, I am often negligent of expressing appreciation to people who give their financial resources. So, I explain:

"You are here, because I want to thank you for 'practicing what I preach' when it comes to stewardship. Our finance office gave me your names as people who appear to be obediently and generously supporting the ministries and vision of our church.

It takes a lot of resources to do what God has called us to do, and I want to do two things. First, I just want to say 'thank you' for your financial support. As your pastor, it is good to know you are 'with us.' Second, I want to share prayer needs with you, about the challenges we are facing as a church. The reason for this is based on what Jesus said. He told us that "Where your treasure is, there your heart will be also" (Matthew 6:21). From this, I assume that your hearts are in the right place, so you are the kind of people I want to have praying for our church."

You must understand, I genuinely mean it! I appreciate such obedient folks, and definitely want them praying for the needs of our church. These people are truly, in light of what Jesus said, putting their "money where their mouth is."

As such, you'd be amazed at the reactions every time we host a 'thank-you dessert.' First, my guests are typically pleasantly surprised. Most will humbly, almost embarrassingly waive off any thanks or credit for giving. They are quick to reply that "We do it for the Lord." At the same time, they show a sense of appreciation for being appreciated. It is no different than if I thank a member of our parking lot team for serving so faithfully, rain or shine. Each of us likes to know our contribution matters to God, and to those who lead us.

...at the same time, they show a sense of appreciation for being appreciated. It is no different than if I thank a member of our parking lot team for serving faithfully, rain or shine. Each of us likes to know our contribution matters to God, and to those who lead us.

Then, as I share prayer needs we are facing as a church and as church leaders, these financial givers become more spiritually vested. I share needs that I often haven't shared publicly. I tell them of plans that are in the works for our future and problems that we are facing. I share personal needs of mine, as well as any being faced by our leadership team. **I am convinced that this has helped raise prayerfulness to a healthier level within our congregation**, among those who support our vision in tangible, quiet ways.

Chapter Five: Practice What You Preach... Personally

While healthy Biblical stewardship needs to be practiced by church leaders as they make decisions for the church, the pastor and other key leaders need to practice the principles in their personal lives as well. Stewardship provides an objective view of obedience unlike any other area of discipleship.

While some of our financial records may be confidential, our financial activity and material priorities are typically very observable to those we lead. Stewardship obedience is more tangibly observable than any other area of the Christian life. While it may be difficult to clearly show how loving or patient a person is, obedience in tithing is pretty objective. Take your income, divide it by 10, and there is no guesswork, you're tithing or you're not. Likewise, you have savings or you don't. You are living without debt, or you're not. The list goes on and on.

> Stewardship obedience is more tangibly observable than any other area of the Christian life...obedience in tithing is pretty objective. Take your income, divide it by 10, and there is no guesswork, you're tithing or you're not.

Like it or not, those in the pews will determine how much they trust you, and whether or not you will be a good steward of their donated funds, by how you model healthy stewardship in your personal life. As pastors and leaders of a congregation, we must model the principles we preach. Here are some practical applications of stewardship in the life of the church leader:

1. **Give generously.** Give beyond the tithe by giving offerings as well. Give in a variety of ways. Give to missions, give to charities fighting urban poverty, give to expansion programs your church has. *Model the generosity you want to see in the congregation you lead.*

2. **Save for the future.** Discipline yourself to put aside funds for future needs. From retirement, to the next refrigerator or set of tires, show the same disciplined planning in your personal financial life that you teach and practice in leading the church.

3. **Live contently within your means.** We live in a consumer society surrounded by messages that all we need is more! Try to model a lifestyle of contentment. Don't get caught up in needing a new automobile every few years (my mid-sized Chevy pickup truck is 9 years old and still looks and runs great). Learn to enjoy what you have, take care of things, repair rather than replace them (when possible), and avoid needing to own the latest and greatest piece of technology, entertainment, and so on. Those you lead will take note if you are practicing what you preach. If not, they trust you less, but when you do, **Trust Grows!**

4. **Avoid Debt.** Saving and planning ahead for purchases, along with learning a lifestyle of contentment, makes avoiding debt possible. Live by the standard, "if we have

to go into debt to have it/do it, we will try to do without." Such debt avoidance will make your life less stressful. You'll be more in control of your decisions and your future (remember, the borrower becomes the lender's slave), and you'll do more with your finances than see them pilfered away through costly interest payments.

It is true that occasional unforeseen catastrophic events can cause unavoidable debt (health crisis, unexpected job loss, an accident, etc.). In these cases, do the best you can, get wise financial guidance, and steer through such seasons of struggle.

However, most debt is indeed avoidable. Over time, as you practice healthy stewardship principles, you will even be able to buy cars with cash. The only loan you'll need is buying a home. I can attest that it is also a great feeling to pay off a house in less than half the time of your mortgage term (something we've been able to do twice). Not only do you save yourself a fortune in interest over the years, you model what you preach, and experience the blessings of obedience.

When making large purchases, like a home or auto, be reasonable and follow these principles, not the advice of finance officers at a bank or car dealership. For instance, we've never wanted to be "house poor." This is a term I've coined, watching others extend themselves so far to buy a home that the financial demands infringe on healthy stewardship and other areas of life.

Each time we have bought a home, the loan officer makes it clear to my wife and I that we could afford a MUCH larger payment (loan) based on both our incomes. We kindly inform them that our priorities are such that we don't want to extend ourselves that far. The same is true when buying vehicles; we can afford more than we typically spend. Let priorities guide you, not what everybody else is doing in our culture.

If you can't afford to tithe because of your house payment, scar payment, or credit card bills, I believe in the words of Malachi: you're robbing God. Don't get caught in this financial, stressful trap. Life will be much better if you steer clear. I also believe you experience more of the blessings of God when we avoid debt, put Him first, practice contentment, and enjoy what Biblical stewardship principles indicate we can afford.

> **Let priorities guide you, not what everybody else is doing.**

Chapter Six: Troubleshooting Possible Explanations for Financial Struggles

This chapter is meant to help church leaders identify potential obstacles to becoming a growing, financially healthy church. This can be a difficult and even painful learning process. If God isn't providing for the financial needs of your church, you may need to ask yourself some difficult questions.

Could there be a disconnect between where or how you are leading your local church, and what God intends? If so, perhaps He is choosing not to provide for your needs intentionally, as a way of painfully getting your attention.

This is a difficult question that definitely could be interpreted as a lack of grace. Financial struggles don't need to be interpreted as God's discipline. However, they often point to something that needs attention.

> When circumstances are clearly identifiable, and out of your control, try to ease up and not panic. Make sound "belt-tightening" decisions, pray fervently and move ahead.

There can be a host of reasons for financial struggle in churches. **Much of the time there are valid explanations that don't point to any problem in direction or leadership.** However, on the other hand, it is presumptuous of us if we never question ourselves, our methods and even our motives. We need to be honest.

Budget-stressors include everything from downturns in the national economy; to financial hardships unique to your community (perhaps a major employer has just left a small town). It may be that in a small church, several families were transferred due to work, and they were mature givers. When circumstances are clearly identifiable, and out of your control, try to ease up and not panic. Make sound "belt-tightening" decisions, pray fervently and move ahead.

However, if your church has chronic financial struggles, it may be for a reason you can indeed discover and address. A few are listed below:

REASONS FOR ONGOING FINANCIAL STRUGGLES IN YOUR CHURCH

1. **Your church is struggling financially because your church isn't growing (as such, your budget isn't growing either).** This is a problem, because expenses always grow, if nothing else, due to inflation. Below are three common reasons why churches don't grow.

    First: You have "leaks" somewhere. Your church can only grow as large or as much as your "weakest characteristic" will allow. If your sanctuary only seats 100 people, you may grow to a few hundred using multiple services on the weekend, but you're limited.

    Response: Identify these limiting characteristics and find solutions! (For a great understanding of this principle, read *Natural Church Development*, by Christian Schwartz.) For example, if you don't have an appealing children's ministry, growth will be difficult if not impossible to achieve or sustain. The list of potential weak spots goes on. Search for such leaks, and if you find them, get to work improving them one step at a time.

    Second: Your church isn't growing due to a lack of a clear, motivating vision. This problem plagues many well

58

intentioned pastors and church leaders. This will be addressed more completely in the final chapter.

Third: Your community isn't growing. In fact, the population may be decreasing. In this case, be the best you can be. Find ways to be an excellent church of your size, in your community. It is likely that even in the smallest communities, a healthy church that meets the relevant needs of people and preaches the hope of Jesus Christ will do well.

Response: Don't compare yourselves to big mega-churches in thriving cities, or even the church across town. *Compare yourself to the standard of simply being an excellent version of you.* Such excellence ranges from the "curb appeal" of the church (who likes to dine in a restaurant that looks run down or poorly maintained outside?) to the quality of ministry for children, and the relevance and impact of the sermons. Likewise, overall friendliness of the congregation is an important factor as well.

2. **Your church is struggling financially because either personally or corporately, you aren't practicing Biblical Stewardship principles, like those explained in this book.** Your failure to follow sound financial practices in your church (intentionally or mistakenly) won't create the kind of trust that encourages people to give freely as they know they should. Likewise, poor financial practices rarely yield efficient results.

Response: Determine which areas are out of compliance. Remedy such practices in your personal life as a leader, as well as corporately in any overall church financial practices that need improvement. Perhaps you need a better method of reporting financial activity to the congregation on an annual basis. Maybe you are too quick to go into debt, either as an individual or a church. Perhaps people are responding to your urgent "special offering" appeals like the boy who cried wolf.

Use this book as a guide. Honestly identify any bad stewardship habits, and begin intentionally correcting them.

Some changes may even be best if you share them with the congregation. For example, you might find it helpful to implement and publicly identify needed changes:

> "We know that our budgeting process has often failed to consider our long term maintenance needs. This year we are going to begin to change this, and as a result, we plan to ask for less 'emergency offerings' for expenses that can honestly be anticipated."

One word of caution: If you make such intentions public, you must follow through with them. Otherwise, you lose even more of the credibility you are trying to earn back. I'll never forget how one member of our church told me I finally earned his "financial trust." I earned it in an announcement I made the weekend before Father's Day, 1992 (some painful memories stay etched in our minds). We 'pulled the plug' on a building program, because we didn't raise the amount of funds we said we wanted in order to move forward. Keep in mind; I had been the lead pastor for about 2 years, after having already served in this church for 7 years before in a

I'll never forget how one member of our church told me I finally earned his "financial trust."

key staff role (which included financial oversight of the budget).

A few years after that announcement in 1992, a long-time attendee said to me: "Do you know when I knew I could trust you?" I obviously wanted to know his answer. "When you 'pulled the plug' on the building program a couple years ago, even though you said that was what we would do, I wasn't sure you would do it until you actually did it. That is when I knew you could be trusted."

> His comments underscore the reality that people in your church are listening to your words, but also watching your actions, and evaluating your decisions, in determining if you can be "financially trusted."

His comments underscore the reality that people in your church are listening to your words, watching your actions, and evaluating your decisions in determining if you can be "financially trusted." As Solomon states in Proverbs 22:1 "A good name is to be more desired than great wealth, favor is better than silver and gold." Indeed, earning and sustaining trust among those who give is essential for financial church health.

Your problem may **not** be due to the fact that you don't practice healthy stewardship. It may be because **you don't**

preach what you practice! You may "dot all your I's and cross all your T's" so-to-speak. You may avoid debt, handle money well, and be a great example of living in contentment. But, if you don't regularly preach and teach about stewardship at all levels of your congregation, you'll likely struggle as a church. In the thought line of Romans 10:14 "How will people know and practice good, Godly stewardship, if someone doesn't teach them?"

People will only practice what you preach, or less. Certainly, if you aren't preaching it, you can't expect it.

3.   **Your church is struggling financially because you don't have a compelling vision to give toward.** This is a key to church financial health, and the focus of the next and final chapter. It is an enduring truth that people who give, want the money they give to go toward something great!

Chapter Seven: Provision Follows Vision

Having established that "God will provide for what He calls us to do," let's re-state it: Provision follows vision. A compelling "God-Sized Vision" will help motivate people to give, not just out of obedience (I *should* do this) but in expectation of what God will do (I *want* to do this.) Christians find joy and fulfillment saying "yes" and giving to something greater than themselves.

MIXED EMOTIONS DISCLAIMER about this chapter *I have been blessed to lead a good sized church. Not an elite mega-church of multiple thousands by any means. Still, CLC is not the average church in America either. We currently have over 2,000 people in attendance on a weekend, including the people at three satellite congregations, each about a 30 minute drive from our original campus.*

> I am a firm believer that "provision follows vision." In essence, if God is leading your church in a direction, He will provide for it.

With that said, my fear with this chapter is that it will be misinterpreted as either "bragging on our accomplishments" or that it will discourage pastors of smaller churches and be dismissed as "advice that only works for larger congregations."

I'll trust that the earlier chapters were helpful enough that the reader will trust the motive behind this chapter. Throughout this chapter, I'll cite our experiences as a testimony of what once would have been WAY beyond our hopes and dreams. To be honest, I know many churches larger than us who are WAY more effective in financial stewardship than we have been. They inspire us, and offer a great example to learn from. Comparatively, we still have a long way to go.

So if you lead a smaller church, as you read any of the stories and just "drop some zeroes." For our church, a project may seem big at $100,000. For your situation, it may be a Goliath at $1,000. The amount is relative, the truth that "God will provide for what He calls us to" is not.

I am a firm believer that "provision follows vision." In essence, if God is leading your church in a direction, He will provide for it. I have also seen that Christians truly want to be part of something bigger than them. I believe they want to give to a vision bigger than themselves, in both their time and their finances. After all, we have been redeemed by the creator of the universe, to accomplish His plans to reach mankind.

> **For our church, a project may seem big at $100,000. For your situation, it may be a Goliath at $1,000. The amount is relative, the truth that "God will provide for what He calls us to" is not.**

At our church, we are convinced that such a calling is bigger than anything we could do on our own (If we can do it alone, the vision isn't big enough!).I am convinced that a compelling vision is essential for being a healthy, growing church...including a financially healthy church!

I have seen such a correlation between vision and giving over the **years that it must be addressed separately in this final chapter.** *Many pastors and church leaders don't realize that YOU as the leader of your church must be the first person to believe this without question. If you don't really believe God will provide, others won't follow.*

The ancient Israelites are a good example of a lack of faith. In spite of all that God had done for them, they doubted Him and complained at every turn. Moses, their leader, was of a different mindset. He knew God could be trusted and God would provide. Whether it was providing guidance by day or night (cloud, fire), shoes that wouldn't wear out, or mysterious manna for their "daily bread" Moses was confident that where God would lead them, he would provide for them too. Can you imagine the mess the Israelites would have been in if Moses was as uncertain of God's faithful provision as the Israelites were that he led?

In so many ways, the Bible makes it clear: *God will provide for what He calls us to do.* This is evidenced in the Old and New Testament. You must be a modern day leader who also believes that "Where God leads you (your church), He will provide.

Admittedly, the unexpected divine "manna-like" miracle is nice. I can testify that they do still happen today! A few years ago, we had a "manna-like" miracle when God provided $100,000 to finish the landscaping of a huge addition to our building. We were out of money and just couldn't afford to complete the landscaping as we originally planned. We had a choice to make, give $100,000 to provide 300,000 fortified rice meals to our partners in Africa, or re-direct the funds to the landscaping. For us, the decision was clear—rice, not shrubs.

Shortly after the decision was finalized, I received a letter from an attorney about a grant from an estate specifically targeted for church facility needs. We received the $100,000 from the estate of a man who, to my knowledge, never even visited our church! God provided it through totally unexpected means!

Such "Miraculous Provision" doesn't condone fiscal presumption that any decision church leaders make will be divinely subsidized. You must indeed clearly **Discern**, **Define**, **Declare** and then **Do** the vision God gives you; but once you have a clear sense of direction, the leader and leadership team must be convinced that God will provide for what He calls you to accomplish.

There are several Biblical examples below of how God provided for the needs of the vision he placed before His people. Lest we get the wrong idea and think God always "drops provision from the sky," you'll notice that unlike the unusual and miraculous provision of manna, (or courtyard landscaping grants) these illustrations show how God typically provides for His work **through** His people.

> Lest we get the wrong idea, and think God always "drops provision from the sky"…God typically provides for His work **through** His people.

The tabernacle is a good example of how God provided through His people for what He intended to do. In Exodus, the Israelites were called to build the Tabernacle as a place of worship during their wilderness journey. Chapter 36 raises a wonderful problem. The leaders came to Moses and said "The people are bringing much more than enough for the construction which the Lord commanded us to perform." (Exodus 36:5 NASB) Moses had to issue a "restraining order" for the people to *stop* giving to construct the tabernacle. *God will provide for what He calls us to do.*

The temple is another example of God providing through His people. Four hundred and eighty years after the people of Israel left Egypt, God led Solomon to build the temple as a permanent house of worship. I Kings 6 describes the elaborate construction project which used everything from hand-hewn cedar from Lebanon, to quarried stones and fine gold overlay. The chapter concludes that it took 7 years to complete the project. Once again we learn, *God will provide for what He calls us to do.*

> **Ideally, people want to give to make an eternal difference in the lives of people, for God's sake.**

God provided through the church for the missions work of Paul. On many occasions Paul reached out to members of the New Testament churches to receive missions offerings to support the spread of the Gospel. In Philippians 4: 18, he celebrates (as every missionary hopes to) by declaring "I received everything in full and have abundance; I am amply supplied..." (Philippians 4:18). Paul encourages those who give, in verse 19, reminding them that God will in turn supply all their needs. From the Old Testament to the New, it is shown repeatedly: *God will provide for what He calls us to do.*

The Bible makes it clear God is interested in providing for our personal needs as we serve Him. Whether it is one of the most unique catering opportunities in history to meet the needs of the prophet Elijah; "I have commanded the ravens to provide for you there..." in 1 Kings 17:4; or the simple promise from Jesus that our heavenly Father will take care of us, "for your heavenly Father knows that you need all these things (food, clothing, shelter)" Matthew 6:32, *God will provide for what He calls us to do.*

We could go on tirelessly citing God's faithful provision through the centuries. Suffice it to say, *God will provide for what He calls us to do.* The reason for this redundant citation is to make this point clear.

As a leader, learn to **Discern Define**, **Declare** and **Do** the vision God has for your church. As the vision grows, you'll find God provides in awesome ways!

Learn to call people to follow and give toward a compelling "God-Sized Vision" as Jesus did. He modeled this idea for us. He called people to give their lives to something great. Think about it, *he invited his listeners to become citizens of the Kingdom of Heaven! Peter, James and John left their nets at the invitation to become "Fishers of men." He bid people not just to a belief system, but to follow him in a life of sacrifice and purpose that led them to a home in heaven.*

Likewise, **Jesus called people to give their money to something beyond themselves.** He wasn't just telling people to give to support His earthly ministry (although to us, in hindsight, that would be great!); He told people that when they gave, they gave to the Kingdom of Heaven.

Sadly, too often, Christianity is diluted down into a life of "hanging on until heaven" or living more aware of what you shouldn't do, than the adventure you can begin at the bidding of the God and creator of the universe. I heard a speaker explain this perspective once to a group of pastors who were complaining about their church members giving huge financial gifts to a popular para-church, television ministry. The point was simply made, and holds true: **people want to give to something greater than themselves. Ideally, people want to give to make an eternal difference in the lives of people, for God's sake.**

This makes perfect practical sense as well. Think about your own life. Most of us aren't nearly as excited about going to the grocery store to buy groceries as we are to eat dinner at a great restaurant. We know the basics need to be tended to, but we really like to invest and be part of a greater experience.

With this understood, how motivated do you suppose people are, when they give to your church? When you consider those who are tithing, do you suppose it is with a sense of purpose, or duty?

Likewise, I am a firm believer that "provision follows vision." In essence, if God is leading your church in a direction, He will provide for it. I have also seen that Christians truly want to be part of something bigger than themselves, both in their time and their finances.

After all, we have been redeemed by the creator of the universe, to accomplish His plans to reach mankind. At our church, we are convinced that such a calling is bigger than anything we could do on our own (If we can do it alone, the vision isn't big enough!). I am convinced that a compelling vision is essential for being a healthy, growing church...including a financially healthy church!

With this understood, how motivated do you suppose people are, when they give to your church? Not to overstate the point, but **when the offering is being received at your church, do you suppose people feel like their contribution is changing lives, transforming urban poverty, and reaching around the world, or just paying the light bill for the church?** Which would you prefer to give to?

> **After all, we have been redeemed by the creator of the universe, to accomplish His plans to reach mankind.**

Since we have developed a "Stewardship culture" motivated by our "God-Sized Vision" we have experienced vision-related financial "miracles" that may seem either large or small compared to your church; for us, they were huge and previously unheard of.

1. We have invested hundreds of thousands of dollars in several inner-city churches in our area to grow their impact on our city.

2. We have launched three satellite campuses from our original campus. Even though startup and equipment costs over $100,000 we can pay cash for such ventures.

3. We have built 3 holistic church communities in Swaziland, Africa to address the poverty and AIDS crisis there. For $125,000 each, we build a church, a pastor's home, and a duplex to offer orphan care to the most needy in the community. We also provide sustainability to these communities with animals and gardens. We pay $20,000 a year for the first two years to "get them going", then they are self-sustaining after that. All of this is paid in cash, through the stewardship of our church.

> I am convinced that a compelling vision is essential for being a healthy, growing church...including a financially healthy church!

4. We are now launching out beyond Swaziland, and are planning to build three such communities in Zambia. In addition, we hope to continue to build an "ICBC" (ICBC: In Community By Community transformational church) in Swaziland every other year. Again, all in cash.

5. We built a 30,000 square foot addition to our original campus for approximately $3 million and paid cash for it.

Now, I know the Skeptic is arguing, "All that vision talk is good, but for our church there is a certain amount of 'overhead' in ministry you can't avoid. Utility bills have to be paid, salaries need to be met, and mortgages need to be current." *All this is true, but there are three things you must do regarding the financial stewardship of the vision God has for your church.* I believe that if you tend to the vision of your church, God will take care of the "overhead" too!

THE THREE ESSENTIAL THINGS THAT MUST BE DONE FOR PROVISION TO FOLLOW VISION: Below are keys to experiencing the provision God has in store for your church.

> I believe that if you tend to the vision of your church, God will take care of the "overhead" too!

First: You must have a compelling vision for your church. I know this sounds obvious, but I can speak from experience. I led Christian Life Center for many years having a sense of vision, but not having anywhere near the clarity of vision for it to be as compelling as visions can be.

Most churches have a mission statement. Ours is "To Know God, Be His People, Value Others, and Change Our World." A mission statement is a good thematic sentence that identifies your 'reason for being.' A vision statement answers the question, "OK, so what does the mission look like as it is becoming reality?"

Many churches have mission statements, vision statements, or both, and they can even feel inspiring. Sadly, however, many churches have a great 'mission statement' that doesn't really correlate with reality. I've seen many churches adopt the pithy phrase **"Win, Train, Send."** **This is great, but if you can't point to who you are winning, how you** are training them, and where you are sending them (and who is then being 'won' as a result of who was sent), the words are just that...words.

The vision we have been following since 2008 has transformed us as a congregation. Likewise, it has made an amazing difference in other churches that have adopted it. I find that few "cut and paste" visions work from one church to another. Such visions often work with highly gifted leaders of mega-churches, but for the average pastor 'in the trenches,' the solutions "get lost in translation." As a result, pastors and church leaders sincerely try to get a better sense of direction, trying the 'next great thing,' and end up discouraged and frustrated.

Our "God-Sized Vision" is Biblically based, and translates to any congregation. Regardless of the vision you choose to pursue as a church, you must pursue and preach it clearly and consistently. Well intended church members get weary with the "passion of the month" when pastors are always switching to a new emphasis. It is difficult to follow a leader who frequently changes course. Likewise, it is difficult to see a vision truly grow, if it is always changing.

> Well intended church members get weary with the "passion of the month..."

I learned this with part of our "God-Sized Vision" which involves a missionary partnership in Swaziland, Africa. Initially, we hoped to build one holistic church community to battle poverty and AIDS in this country of a million people (20% of whom are orphans).

Now, having stayed with that part of our vision for 6 years, we have helped build (and funded) four such communities, not just one. In addition to this, we plan to build dozens more, and have launched out and will begin our first such community in Zambia this year (with a total of three planned for Zambia). Had we changed course, pursued another missions opportunity, we may have built one community, but we would have never gained the consistent momentum to do what we have done in six short years. To God be the glory!

Regardless of the vision you choose for your church, **have one!** Clearly preach it, invest your energies and resources into it, and stay at it. As you begin to see fruits of your labor and focus, celebrate them. Few things will be more encouraging to members of your congregation than hearing stories of changed lives, and a vision becoming reality.

> **Regardless of the vision you choose to pursue as a church, you must pursue it and preach it clearly, and consistently.**

Second: Make sure your vision, and how you allocate your resources, is in line with what reflects the heart of God. I said earlier in this book that I believe "God is an accountability God." When I couple this with the verse in James that says teachers will receive a "stricter judgment" (James 3:1), I am sobered with the responsibility of leading a church. Sometimes I honestly wonder how much the modern church is what Christ had in mind. Since I pastor a contemporary American church, I pray we're consistent with the Lord's desire, even though the world has obviously changed through the centuries of time.

Methods of our ministry have indeed changed. From where we meet, to the technology we use, this is not the New Testament world. However, some things are consistent. The nature of human need remains, and I believe that there are some non-negotiables for those of us who call ourselves Christians. Jesus describes a sobering scene at the final judgment in Matthew 25: 35, 36

> "For I was hungry and you gave me something to eat; I was thirsty and you gave me something to drink; I was a stranger and you invited me in; naked, and you clothed me; I was sick, and you visited me; I was in prison and you came to me."

I refer to this passage as "Basic Christian Compassion." Most of us have these "basic needs" met in life. To provide them for those who lack them is the truest compassion that can be given. Your church MUST have a vision that includes putting resources (both time and money) into Matthew 25 kinds of needs.

For us, we are intentional about making Basic Christian Compassion part of our "DNA" as a church.

For us, we are intentional about making Basic Christian Compassion part of our DNA as a church. For example, we have a clothing ministry that reaches out to our community and provides several tons of clothing each month. We have a food pantry for people in need who are part of our congregation. We provide approximately 2,000 families (about 10,000 people) Thanksgiving dinner each year. Seventy five percent of these meals are distributed through our inner-city partner churches. We have purchased, packaged and sent 1.8 million fortified rice meals to our partners in Africa over the past 5 years; the list goes on.

This kind of compassion also speaks a clear, evangelistically authentic message to our community. In an age when people are "out for themselves" or expect the government to take care of others, we find that non-Christian people respect and appreciate our compassionate efforts (even people who don't receive the help, respect that we do it). It seems to me that when our church has been doing well with Basic Christian Compassion, God provides for these needs and blesses the church overall. Likewise, we often struggle financially a bit more as a church when we get distracted away from helping to meet these needs.

I'm not suggesting compassion for the sake of getting. I'm observing that blessings follow obedience, as Jesus himself said: "Give and it shall be given unto you" (Luke 6:38).

> *This kind of compassion also speaks a clear, evangelistically authentic message to our community.*

One word of caution about Basic Chrisitan Compassion. It is important that compassion be given to genuinely help an individual in need. The more we work among such folks, we find that there are ways that we can think we are helping them, but we are not. Giving to those truly in need is what Jesus calls us to. *Learn to discern between giving that helps, and giving that enables.* Just giving "handouts" for the sake of someone asking, and us feeling better for having obliged is often anything but compassionate. A great book to read in this regard is: *Toxic Charity* by Robert Lupton.

Third: Declare the vision often and celebrate accomplishments regularly. I believe Bill Hybels is the person who reminds leaders that vision is like pouring water into a bucket with some holes in the bottom and that "vision leaks." The process of **Discerning, Defining,**

Declaring and **Doing** a "God-Sized Vision" is an essential on-going practice for a healthy church, and a financially healthy church.

Suffice it to say, one of the key responsibilities of the Lead Pastor of your church, and the leadership team with them, is to cast vision, then cast it again, then cast it again; because with all the distractions in life, "vision leaks." And when you cast vision, be sure to show people the fruit of their giving and of their effort. This will help affirm that their giving is resourcing this grand Kingdom cause!

> Your responsibility is to communicate this motivating, fruitful message to your church as often as it applies...

When people give, they will assume part of their giving is indeed paying the utility bill since the lights are on and the toilets in the bathroom work. That isn't what is worth celebrating. When they give, show them tangible ways how God is miraculously taking their tangible financial gifts, and transforming them into life change, and heavenly gains. Your responsibility is to communicate this motivating, fruitful message to your church as often as it applies: *"Your giving is directly (or indirectly) making a tangible, Kingdom building, life-changing difference in our community, our region, across the nation, or around the world!"*

I'll share another recent example. We are in the midst of a building campaign. After several years of needing a larger sanctuary at our original campus , we have agreed to demolish our 33 year old sanctuary to rebuild one on the same location that is about 3 times the size. Our plans are to build and pay for the new sanctuary over a 5 year period.

Here is where **celebrating accomplishments** comes in. As part of the expansion and our vision, we took the pews from the former sanctuary (that are still in really good shape) and did an "Extreme Makeover" with four of our inner-city partner churches. About 80 volunteers from our church joined forces with volunteers from these churches. We painted their sanctuaries, replaced carpet, and retrofitted the pews to their sanctuaries. The whole project took about two months.

On installation day, we had video cameras busy, and we have shown a few clips of the work being done and the amazing transformations for our inner city partners. Every time we show these videos, we vehemently thank our congregation for their giving. We thank them for making a pledge to our expansion project. And we remind them that their giving to our church is making an exciting, tangible difference across our city!

> ...people assume part of their giving is indeed paying the utility bills. That isn't what is worth celebrating...

This isn't manipulation; it is truth. Our vision as a church is indeed much more than what happens within our walls. God IS using us to make a difference in the needs across our city, but also around the world, even in poverty stricken and AIDS ridden Swaziland, Africa. The effectiveness of the vision is what helps motivate people to give. Whether a person from our church returns from a missions trip to Africa, or a day downtown at an urban-partner outreach, their common response to me is..."Pastor Stan, it's WORKING!"

Let me tell you, *that* kind of fruitfulness gives people the realization that what they gives matters! It matters to our church, it matters to churches across our inner city, and it matters to widows and orphans in Africa! I am convinced people would rather give their hard-earned tithes to a church that is helping make a difference across their city and around the world, than to answer pleas for giving "so we can repair cracks in the asphalt in the parking lot."

Don't be defeated or discouraged. Jesus has called us to be the light of the world! God has a vision for your church. Prayerfully **Discern** what it is. **Define** it. Then, as you consistently **Do** it, remember it is also your responsibility to **Declare** this motivating, fruitful message to your church as often as it applies:

> **"Your giving is directly (or indirectly) making a tangible, Kingdom building, life-changing difference in our community, our region, across the nation, or around the world. Oh yeah, and by-the-way, we'll pay to keep the lights on too."**

Our vision as a church is indeed much more than what happens within our walls.

Today, many churches are struggling financially. Likewise, there are many pastors and church leaders who don't know how to lead a financially healthy church. Also, finances are sensitive issues in the church today. This book can be used as a resource to manage them effectively.

Learn the *key principles and practices* of financial health. Here are a few discussed in this book:

- Choosing the right response to financial struggles is critical
- Intentionality is a key success factor for a financially healthy church
- The heart of financial health is not about money

This book is intended to help churches become financially healthy, so they can be free to pursue their "God-sized" visions in our world.

A key premise of this book is that financial health is both a blessing and a result of proper practices for individuals and churches.

Stan Tharp has over 35 years of ministry experience and has served as the lead pastor of Christian Life Center (CLC) for nearly 25 years. He holds an M.A. in Pastoral Counseling and Psychology, an M.B.A. in Management, and a D. Min in Conflict Management. He currently resides in Dayton, OH with his wife, Joyce, and their two children. He is also the author of *BIG* and *Teach Them To Give*.

Visit his website to learn more:
stantharp.wordpress.com

ISBN 9781500343736

SCHOLASTIC

Tickety Toc

TRIPLE TROUBLE TIME

This book belongs to:

_____

_____